FLIGHTS OF FANTASY

POETRIES

OINDRILA NANDI

The book has been dedicated to all those amazing people i have met and from whom i have learnt the meaning of life , and those I havent met but wish to meet somewhere in a blank space of land where theres nothing wrong or right. Untill then, lets begin here.....

Contents

Foreword

Poetry for ....

This issue is an amalgamation of everything that is dear to me ,my thoughts, my lifes experiences and hardships that i have faced and facing through.We have printed some beautiful poems in this edition that revolves around the practice of mutual understanding between individuals. The possible endings are made on the readers end to derive and imagine. Some of the poems have endings that has been marked vividly by the lifes happening.

Preface

Giving an introduction to thy self can never be satisfying enough,as I feel we all along with who we actually are try to possess and replicate certain traits of homosapiens that we love to be or imagine to become. Nevertheless finishing my grad school degree from a reputed girls college in Kolkata, went to fly high in the sky for few years....and once i landed back to my homeland got myself hitched into a loving family.

The inspiration of writing poems has been my life. I always had this secret admiration towards poetry in general ,as i found the way to be the most eloquent and mesmerizing way of telling your thoughts.Every journey of a soul comes with its share of ups and downs which I like to call as lessons learnt and learnings: without which life becomes boring. Taking matter as it comes and not always at your stride is something that requires time to learn. For me, writing poems is the way i can show the world about my learnings and enrich someone elses lessons.

Gratitude....

Acknowledgements

To my darling husband,

Chapter 1

<u>**Into the light**</u>

I sleep on the bed with open eyes,
Breathing frantically but ghastly deep;
Itap my fingers one and two,
Thinking vaguely and momentarily.
A sound comes in from far and near,
high and low Iget a fear;
Oh! Isnt it the calling of the master there,-I stage. He glanced at
me at a staring glaze,
The melanchony voice of a human race,
It stays all over and everywhere:melows down in the nights
affair.
I blink ,blink,blink and blink......
Thinking hard of all blossom and pink.
And then just as I flitter my eye lash,
Isee the world with a lighting flash;
Joys,sorrows and spirits high,
Up I see on the sky...
To the end with my utter dismay,
How fake and uncanny the world is may,
I close my eyes in this belief,
Let the arms be open and arrows unleash;

In the world spread thee love and peace,
that will have no worries and boundaries , till the end I see.

Chapter2

<u>Rise</u>

A ranged spell, at a perfect encounter,

to dismiss all in the battelfield;

I come here to rise and rise......

Including the skeleton army and the marching troops.

The ability of falling and rising up,

marking the pointer at the board;

Falling carelessly and rising fearlessly,

spirits go up and adored.

I hear again the voice of rise and rise....

The use of cards in the game of life,

Win or loose is hard to say.....as almost all complys to play;

To hit the low you got to see,

The high rays from the bark of the tree,

to dismiss the skelly in despair,

move forward in the light of rise and uprear.

3. Chapter 3

<u>*To My-*</u>

The look on the face is hard to bear,
Wrinkles on the forehead says it all;
Wondering frantically here and there,
Where is my petal gone in despair......!!
The laugh and cry of the cheeks,
mumbling words on the lips;
The winds of overcast are gripping,
Into the ocean , drops are plopping;
My love, here I now come to you,
no flower or thorn or pouring cloud;
Can clasp me from flocking about,
If its not now , then it will never be then;
all kisses are left,
all pain in vain;
As the ocean waves sways on its shore,
I plant my kiss onto your facetious pore.

Chapter4

<u>Death</u>

Before and after is a state of mind,
A music echoes in the ear;
notes sinking and whirling in the dwine,
heart pounding up in fear.
The first drop of rain on the Earth,
The smell of soil and dust;
In my thoughts Isee what we lost and gone,
Love itself withholds on....
What is death ,I ask in dismay....!
It comes across and offers pray,
The smell of the beloved lying on the bed,
nothing moving lives us dead.....
Of spirits move and leaves us pain stricken,
and thats how death is forgiven.

Chapter5

<u>**Lilly**</u>

Love my Lilly,
her voice silly,
All things are divine,
She rises and shine.
Music and Dance appears as they,
Now and then she remains in sway;
Her hands and legs are rythimically curved,
with perfect shade of pink paved.....
The twinkling of her eyes ,
and stroke of her lip line;
needs no ties,
or light it can be-
Arrival of her makes the orchids bloom;
and departure makes the day go gloom.
Tonight we will watch from dawn to dusk,
into the river and over podcast,
I sing and dance and say silly Lilly-
here I stand yours only Billy.

Chapter6

The Bride

Autumn is the time of the year,

leaves fall from trees scatters everywhere;

From pleasant wind to chilly jitters,

In the wintermonth the bride to be-glitters..

Be it gold,diamond or silver streaks,

The bride to be blushes as she speaks;

The time has come to the Day,

when the adrenaline rush is at its peak,

asking for the time to sneak......

All that I hoped for,and eveything I dreamed to be,

is coming to a closure, as fast as it can be;

And now I am ready to go to the world,

with bright smile and an open chord;

All the precious moments I led and those coming my bay,

I welcome them all in a benevolent way.

Chapter 7

<u>***Rewind and Replay***</u>

Life is all about learn and play,
Be it night or day;
We learn things to do,
Merry tones we sing impromptu;
Rewind, Play and Pause are the key notes of the game,
Thats how we watch our step in fame and shame.

Chapter8

<u>*Notion of life*</u>

Fun to give,

Fun to get;

Joy to give,

Joy to get;

In this world of busy bees,

Some wonderful people are The chosen one to be;

Love to give,

Love to get;

is all that is wanted to live and introspect.

Chapter9

Calling you

A word that comes often and say-"is tone of Hello" !!
The light of the lamp dims away;
The pillow falls from the rocking chair,
profundly I get up and lash a spear.
Days cross by and nights never end,
All that I hear is the word that comes often.
Admist of bombing, blasting and crashing sound,
I fear all time-are we lost or found;
Oh dear! the past is holding back ,
Into the world of gravitational pull;
I try to break bars and come tough,
not mess up and be rough.
But still somewhere ago I saw,
Someone calling me ashore....
Across the sea, in the moonlight
I hear thou voice calling me aside.

Chapter 10

<u>**My Dearest you-**</u>

I sit down with a desire to write,
My life swings with cloudy strides;
As time draws different lines,
I sit and think what is underlined;
The lush green of grasses and vineyards,
Tells my heart to beat a thousand yards;
Oh my beloved, my soul engulfs,
Love thy heart never halts apart.
Presence is not felt ny the presence of thee,
But presence is felt by the absence of thy....
I smile and cry when am all alone,
Love conquers all in the game unknown;
Now that I am not anymore,
smile a while shed a tear-
show the love to all who you care,
To be yours is to be you,
All that blooms fall and rise-
Is why I Love you till every sunrise.

Chapter11

<u>Roses</u>

Roses are mine ,
So are you;
Roses are divine,
So are you.
Roses are red,
Kisses turn blue;
Hugs are send,
To be with you.
If smile is a petal,
I send you a bouquet;
If love is a spirit,
I send you my soul.

Acknowledgements

I would like to thank my partner for inspiring me in writing these poems,along with my beautiful daughter who constantly dragged me in giving my best. Along with them a special word for my parents without whose constant help the work would have been undone.

Nevertheless thanks to all the readers who constanly inspire me to write better and believe in me and my work,a special note of gratitude to all of you.

14.06.22